Introduction

When you look at your Christmas tree, which ornaments stand out the most? Chances are they are handmade, either by you or a loved one.

The best thing about handmade ornaments is the memories that come with them—there is nothing better than reminiscing about past holidays spent with loved ones. This year, why not create more memories by hand-making the ornaments in this book? You can make them as gifts, or get the whole family involved and spend the afternoon crafting.

We've included a wide variety of designs from traditional to whimsical for the very young to the young-at-heart, and even for a favorite pet. Many of the ornaments are easy to make and can be made in an hour or two using general supplies found in local sewing and craft stores. If you have a stash of sewing and craft supplies, this will be a wonderful way to make good use of what you have on hand.

Don't stop with making Christmas ornaments! You can also be creative by using these designs to make gift tags, hot pads, cards, coasters or mug rugs. If you enjoy making ornaments, but your list is small, make ornaments by the batch to sell at a craft bazaar, or better yet, bring a smile to someone in need by giving handmade Christmas ornaments to your favorite charity.

May you have lots of fun making Christmas ornaments that your family and friends will cherish for many years to come.

To download templates for easy printing, go to: *AnniesCatalog.com/customers/check_code.html* and enter 151064

Table of Contents

Traditional Trimmings continued

Holiday Sentiments, **31**

Patchwork Star, **32**

Beaded Patchwork, **34**

Candy Cane Stocking, **36**

Christmas Critters

Weiner Wonderland, **37**

Little Rudolf, **38**

Perky Penguin, **40**

Give Me a Paw, **48**

Tweetie Bird, **42**

Mouse in a Mitten, **44**

Holiday Ponies, **47**

Winter Wonderland

Snowman Trio, **50**

Baby's First Christmas, **52**

Mr. & Mrs. Snowman, **54**

Mr. Flurry, **56**

Thready Freddy, **59**

Snowflake Duo, **60**

Let It Snow, **62**

Marvin the Melting Snowman, **58**

Clothesline Christmas Tree & Bell

Designs by Chris Malone

Finished Sizes
Tree: 4½ x 5½ inches
Bell: 4 x 6 inches

Christmas Tree

Materials
- ¾-inch-wide fabric strips:
    Total of 12 inches red
    Total of 65 inches green
- 48 inches of ³⁄₁₆-inch-diameter cotton
  clothesline rope
- Buttons:
    1 (1-inch-diameter) yellow
    3 (⅝-inch-diameter) red
- 8-inch piece of yellow pearl cotton or other
  thin cord
- Tacky fabric adhesive
- Basic sewing tools and equipment

Assembly
1. Apply a drop of adhesive to the end of the wrong side of a red fabric strip.

2. Place the rope end on the glue. Fold the excess fabric over the top and the side of the rope. Spiral wrap the fabric strip around the rope at an angle so each wrap overlaps the previous wrap by at least ¼ inch (Figure 1). Keep the fabric snug against the rope.

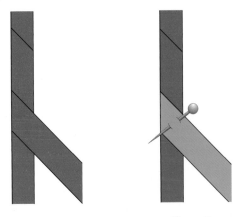

Figure 1   Figure 2

3. Wrap 7 inches of the rope, clip off any excess fabric and glue fabric end to the rope.

4. Apply a drop of glue to the end of the wrong side of a green strip. Overlap the red strip end with the green and press in place. Use a pin to hold the junction until the glue sets (Figure 2).

5. Wrap 18 inches of rope with green fabric strips; secure the end with a dot of glue and a pin.

6. Coil the red-wrapped rope end into a tight circle to the junction of the red and green fabric.

7. Straight-stitch an "X" across the circle to hold the coils in place (Figure 3).

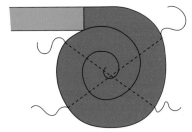

Figure 3

8. Set your sewing machine to a ¼-inch-wide zigzag stitch. Position the center of the coiled shape under the presser foot. Zigzag stitch between the coils catching two coils in each stitch (Figure 4). *Note: To stitch the coils, stop stitching often with the needle down and turn the coil slightly before resuming stitching.*

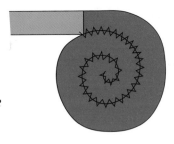

Figure 4

9. Backstitch to secure the coil stitching at the green wrapped section; remove the coil from the machine. Change the thread on the machine to green.

10. To shape the tree, extend the rope tail at a right angle to the coiled base. Turn the rope back on itself making a 2-inch tight loop.

11. Zigzag-stitch the two green rows together beginning at the color junction. Stop stitching with the needle down in the upper rope referring to

Figure 5. Raise the presser foot and turn the ornament 180 degrees.

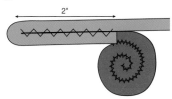

Figure 5

12. Pull the rope tail straight down and turn it back on itself 2 inches from the junction of the two colors to complete the first row.

13. Pull the rope back almost to the first loop and fold it back on itself (Figure 6). Zigzag together.

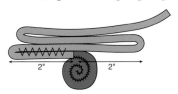

Figure 6

14. Continue to fold the rope back and forth, creating steadily shorter rows to form the triangular tree shape.

15. Add more fabric strips as necessary; overlap and glue fabric ends together to add another fabric strip.

16. At the top of the tree, clip any excess rope and fabric, tucking the fabric tip inside. Backstitch to secure the zigzag stitches (Figure 7).

17. Stitch the yellow star button to the top front of the tree and three red buttons to the center of the tree referring to the sample photo.

Figure 7

18. To make a hanger, thread a needle with yellow cord. Take a small stitch on the back of the tree at the top and tie the ends in a knot.

Bell

Materials
- ¾-inch-wide fabric strips:
  Total of 12 inches of yellow
  Total of 90 inches of green
- 65 inches of ³⁄₁₆-inch-diameter cotton clothesline rope
- 1 (¾-inch-diameter) red button
- 8-inch piece of red pearl cotton or other thin cord
- Tacky fabric adhesive
- Basic sewing tools and equipment

Assembly
1. Follow Christmas Tree assembly steps 1–5 using the yellow and green strips.

2. Coil the yellow-wrapped end into a tight, slightly oval shape. Straight stitch an X across the circle to hold the coils in place, referring to Figures 3 and 4.

3. Follow Christmas Tree assembly steps 8 and 9 to finish the yellow section of rope.

4. Shape the bell referring to Christmas Tree assembly steps 10–15.

5. At the top of the bell, trim away any excess leaving a 2-inch tail of green-wrapped rope. Coil the 2-inch tail into a tight circle and finish the stitching referring to Figure 7.

6. Sew the red button to the top of the bell.

7. Make a hanger with the red cord referring to Tree ornament step 18. ■

Hexagon Wreath

Design by Tie Dye Diva Patterns

Finished Size
6-inch diameter

Materials
- 6 coordinating 3-inch square dark green print scraps
- 6 coordinating 3-inch square light green print scraps
- Polyester fiberfill
- 5-inch piece of ¼–½-inch-wide ribbon
- Purchased satin bow
- Basic sewing supplies and equipment

Cutting
Use pattern provided on insert. Transfer all markings to fabric.

From print scraps:
- Cut 12 hexagons.

Assembly
Stitch right sides together using a ¼-inch seam allowance unless otherwise indicated.

1. Stitch two dark green hexagons together along one edge (Figure 1); press seam open. Stitch six dark green hexagons together in a circle. Do not join the first and last hexagons.

Figure 1

2. Repeat step 1 with six light green hexagons for wreath back.

3. Stitch wreath front and back together around inside and outside edges matching raw edges (Figure 2). Pivot at corners and leave open between first and last hexagons.

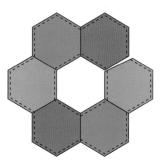

Figure 2

4. Turn wreath right side out through opening; press well.

5. Stuff wreath lightly with fiberfill. ***Note:*** *Use the eraser end of a pencil to push fiberfill toward center of wreath.*

6. Stitch across the seams between hexagons to give the wreath a quilted look referring to Figure 3.

Figure 3

7. Finger-press the raw edges of the last hexagon ¼ inch to the inside. Insert the raw edges of the first hexagon into last hexagon and hand-stitch to secure.

8. Stitch hanging loop and purchased bow over hand-stitched seam to complete. ■

Yo-Yo Tree & Wreath

Designs by Margie Ullery

Finished Sizes
Tree: 3½ x 5 inches
Wreath: 5 inches diameter

Yo-Yo Tree

Materials
- 3½-inch square gold tonal
- 3½-inch square brown print
- 12-inch square green print
- Matching all-purpose thread
- 17 total blue, green and gold micro-minibuttons
- 1 gold star button
- 10-inch red ribbon or woven trim
- Basic sewing supplies and equipment

Assembly
1. To make yo-yos, cut six 2¼-inch-diameter circles from green print and one each from gold tonal and brown print.

2. Finger-press ¼ inch around the circle's outer edge to the wrong side. Hand-stitch in place around the circle taking a backstitch at the beginning to secure the thread as shown in Figure 1.

Figure 1

3. Gently pull the thread, tightly gathering the outer edge toward the center of the circle referring again to Figure 1.

4. Knot the thread ends to secure the gathered edge and trim.

5. Flatten the circle with the gathered edge on the right side to complete the yo-yo as shown in Figure 1.

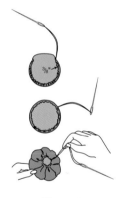

6. Hand-stitch yo-yos together in tree shape referring to Figure 2. Stitch colored micro-mini buttons on tree for lights.

Figure 2

7. Fold ribbon or woven trim in half and attach to back of tree for hanger.

Yo-Yo Wreath

Materials
- 12-inch square green print
- 8 micro-mini red buttons
- 10-inch red ribbon or woven trim
- Basic sewing supplies and equipment

Assembly
1. Make eight 1⅛-inch-diameter green print yo-yos referring to steps 1–5 of Yo-Yo Tree instructions.

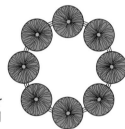

2. Hand-stitch yo-yos together referring to Figure 3. Stitch red micro-mini buttons on wreath for berries.

Figure 3

3. Fold ribbon or woven trim in half and attach to back of tree for hanger. ■

Tree-mendous Threesome

Designs by Linda Miller

Triangle Tree

Finished Size
Approximately 5 x 6½ inches

Materials
- Scraps plaid homespuns
- ⅛ yard Osnaburg
- All-purpose thread to match fabrics
- 2 yards green string
- Polyester fiberfill
- 5 (⅝-inch) red buttons
- Basic sewing supplies and equipment

Assembly
Stitch right sides together using a ¼-inch seam allowance unless otherwise indicated.

Use pattern provided on insert. Transfer all markings to fabric.

1. Cut one Osnaburg and two plaid homespun 1½ x 3-inch rectangles for tree trunk.

2. Layer the trunk pieces wrong sides together with Osnaburg between; stitch around sides and bottom.

3. Stuff polyester fiberfill between two of the layers; stitch to close opening.

4. Cut 10 homespun and five Osnaburg Triangle Tree triangles.

5. Repeat steps 2 and 3 with two plaid homespun and one Osnaburg triangle, leaving a 2-inch opening on the bottom edge for stuffing.

6. Repeat step 5 to make five stuffed triangles.

7. Place the long side of one triangle between the tops of two triangles as shown in Figure 1; pin to hold.

Figure 1

8. Place the long sides of the two bottom triangles from step 7 between the two remaining triangles, again referring to Figure 1; pin to hold.

9. Place one button on each side of center triangles at tips and stitch through all layers and the buttons on both sides as shown in Figure 2. Repeat with two bottom triangles.

Figure 2   **Figure 3**

10. Center and insert the stuffed trunk piece between the two bottom triangles as shown in Figure 3; stitch to hold in place.

11. Cut green string to make two equal lengths.

12. Create a hanging loop and bow from one length of green string and attach to the top tree triangle with remaining button.

13. Cut remaining green string in half and make two bows. Hand-stitch one bow to each side of tree bottom just above trunk.

Tree-mendous Threesome
Triangle Tree Ornament
Placement Diagram approximately 5" x 6½"

Layered Tree

Finished Size
Approximately 6 x 5½ inches

Materials
- Scraps plaid homespuns
- ⅛ yard Osnaburg
- All-purpose thread to match fabrics
- 1 yard green string
- Polyester fiberfill
- 2 (⅜-inch) red buttons
- 1 red star button
- Spray bottle and water
- Toothbrush
- Basic sewing supplies and equipment

Assembly
Stitch right sides together using a ¼-inch seam allowance unless otherwise indicated.

Use patterns provided on insert. Transfer all markings to fabric.

1. Cut one large homespun Layered Tree pattern from homespun for backing and one of each remaining size from homespun and Osnaburg.

2. Cut one Osnaburg and two plaid homespun 1½ x 3-inch rectangles for tree trunk.

3. Prepare tree trunk as in steps 2 and 3 for the Triangle Tree.

4. Pin an Osnaburg shape on the wrong side of each same-size plaid homespun shape.

5. Layer the pinned shapes, starting with the largest and ending with the smallest, as shown in Figure 4; stitch around each shape through all layers, starting with smallest shape in center.

Figure 4

6. Spritz and brush to create a rag texture.

7. Place the stitched unit wrong sides together with the backing piece; stitch leaving a 2-inch opening in the bottom.

8. Insert the trunk piece into the opening and baste to one edge.

9. Stuff with polyester fiberfill and stitch the opening closed.

10. Create a loop with approximately 1-inch ends at the top edge using green string. Sew the red star button to the tree top over loop ends.

11. Sew two ⅜-inch red buttons to the center of the smallest triangle to complete the ornament.

Tree-mendous Threesome
Layered Tree Ornament
Placement Diagram approximately 6" x 5½"

Chenille Tree

Finished Size
Approximately 4½ x 6½ inches

Materials
- Scraps plaid homespuns
- ¼ yard Osnaburg
- All-purpose thread to match fabrics
- Polyester fiberfill
- 7 (⅜-inch) red buttons
- Spray bottle and water
- Toothbrush
- Fabric glue
- Basic sewing supplies and equipment

Assembly
Stitch right sides together using a ¼-inch seam allowance unless otherwise indicated.

Use pattern provided on insert. Transfer all markings to fabric.

1. Cut five 7-inch squares plaid homespun.

2. Cut one 7-inch square Osnaburg.

3. Cut two 1½ x 3-inch trunk pieces plaid homespun and one Osnaburg.

4. Prepare tree trunk as in steps 2 and 3 for the Triangle Tree.

5. Layer four plaid squares and the Osnaburg square right side up on a flat surface, with the Osnaburg square centered in the layers.

6. Stitch diagonal lines ½ inch apart to cover the entire square as shown in Figure 5.

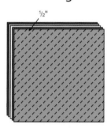

Figure 5

7. Cut down the center between stitching lines through all except the bottom layer as shown in Figure 6.

Figure 6

8. Spritz the square with water and brush with a toothbrush to fringe; let dry.

9. Trace the tree shape on the right side of the remaining plaid homespun square.

10. Place brushed squares wrong sides together with the traced backing square.

11. Stitch on the marked line through all layers, leaving a 2-inch opening in the bottom edge of the tree shape.

12. Trim ¼ inch beyond stitching line as shown in Figure 7.

Figure 7

13. Stuff with polyester fiberfill.

14. Insert the trunk piece into the opening and hand-stitch the opening closed.

15. Cut a 3-inch piece of the cutaway layered-and-stitched section, centering a line of stitching in the piece as shown in Figure 8; fold to make a loop.

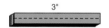

Figure 8

16. Machine-stitch the loop to the top back-side edge of the tree for hanging.

17. Glue a red ⅜-inch button to the tip of each tree branch and tree top to complete the ornament. ■

Tree-mendous Threesome
Chenille Tree Ornament
Placement Diagram approximately 4¹⁄₂" x 6¹⁄₂"

Joy

Design by Chris Malone

Finished Size
6 x 3 inches

Materials
- Small piece felt each green, red and light green
- Standard embroidery floss: green and red
- 10 red E beads
- 20 inches ⅜-inch-wide red transparent ribbon
- Fiberfill stuffing
- Tacky fabric glue (optional)
- Basic sewing tools and equipment

Cutting
Use patterns provided on insert.

From green felt:
- Cut 2 O letters.

From red felt:
- Cut 2 each J and Y letters.

From light green felt:
- Cut 9 holly leaves.

Assembly
All embroidery is worked with two strands of floss.

1. Pin J pieces together and blanket-stitch all around with red floss, lightly stuffing the letter as you stitch. Repeat with Y pieces.

2. Pin and blanket-stitch the wreaths together around the inner circle with green floss. Then stitch around the outer edge, lightly stuffing the wreath as you stitch.

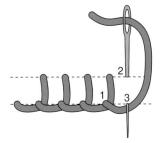

Blanket Stitch

4. Referring to the photo, pin leaves to wreath front in a random fashion and attach each with a single straight stitch down the center with green floss.

5. Position and sew the 10 beads around the wreath as shown, using red floss or thread.

6. Arrange the three pieces as shown with the wreath in front, overlapping the edges of the two letters. Secure with glue or by tacking with thread.

7. Cut off an 8-inch-length from the ribbon; tie in a bow. Glue or tack to the wreath and trim the ends.

8. To make hanger, tie a knot about 1 inch from both ends of the remaining ribbon. Tack ribbon knot to outer front corner of J and Y. ■

Santa & Angel Ornaments

Designs by Chris Malone

Angel With Bell

Finished Size
6½ inches high

Materials
- Scraps light green tonal and pale pink solid
- ⅛ yard white tonal
- Scraps batting
- All-purpose thread to match fabrics
- 1½-inch-diameter wooden disc or rounded button
- 1 yard ⅝-inch-wide red satin ribbon (wire-edge optional)
- 2 (³⁄₁₆-inch) black buttons
- 1 (¾-inch) white button
- 9 (6mm) red beads
- Red beading or quilting thread
- ⅞-inch silver jingle bell
- 4-inch length ⅝-inch-wide silver ribbon
- 8 inches silver cord
- Cosmetic blush and cotton-tip swab
- Fabric glue
- Large-eye embroidery needle
- Basic sewing supplies and equipment

Assembly
Stitch right sides together using a ¼-inch seam allowance unless otherwise indicated.

Use patterns provided on insert. Transfer all markings to fabric.

1. Trace angel body and arm pieces onto wrong side of white tonal, reversing pattern for second arm.

2. Fold fabric in half with drawn lines on top and pin to a scrap of batting.

3. Sew all around traced shapes, leaving top edge open on body; repeat on layered arm pieces, leaving no opening.

4. Cut out each shape ⅛ inch from seam; clip curves.

5. Turn body shape right side out through top opening; press.

6. Machine- or hand-stitch top opening closed, if desired.

7. Cut a slit through one layer only on each arm piece where indicated on pattern; turn arms right side out through the opening and press. Hand-stitch openings closed.

8. Repeat steps 1–6, leaving the square end open, to make two holly-leaf wings.

9. Machine-stitch a vein line down the center of each leaf.

10. To make head, glue batting to top of wooden disc or button; trim to fit.

11. Cut a 3¼-inch-diameter circle from pale pink solid fabric; hand-stitch a line of stitches ⅛ inch from edge all around. Do not cut thread.

12. Place disc, batting side down, on inside of fabric circle; pull thread to gather fabric edges firmly to center back of disc and secure thread.

13. Sew black buttons to face for eyes. Use cotton-tip swab to apply blush to cheeks.

14. Sew red beads to the top and side of head using red beading or quilting thread, taking two stitches for each bead.

15. Glue head to top edge of body front; apply a dot of fabric glue to top of arm and "hand" area; press arm to body front referring to Placement Diagram for positioning. Repeat for second arm.

16. Glue end of holly-leaf wings to back of head.

17. Glue white button to back of head to finish or cover raw edges.

18. Cut an 8-inch piece of red satin ribbon; tie in a bow.

19. Trim ends in a V-cut and glue to body front under face.

20. Starting ¼ inch from one end of the remainder of the ribbon and using 2 strands of matching thread, sew along the length of the ribbon in a zigzag pattern with ½ inch between stitches at

each edge as shown in Figure 1, gathering as you stitch and stopping ¼ inch from end.

Figure 1

21. Pull thread until ribbon fits around angel skirt, about 1 inch up from bottom edge. Glue the ruched ribbon to the skirt, overlapping ends at center back.

22. Thread silver ribbon through the bell hole; tie ends in a double knot. Glue or tack knot to body between hands.

23. Thread cord through large-eye embroidery needle; take a small stitch at top back of head. Remove cord from needle; tie ends in knot and trim close to knot to make hanger to finish.

Santa Ornament

Finished Size
4 x 5¼ inches

Materials
- Scraps 2 coordinating red-and-white prints, white tonal and pale pink solid
- Scrap batting
- All-purpose thread to match fabrics
- White hand-quilting thread
- 2 (¼-inch) black buttons
- 1 (6mm) red bead
- 3 small red E beads
- 9 inches ⅜-inch-wide black velvet ribbon
- ⅝-inch red star button with shank removed
- 5 inches mini holly garland
- 8 inches red cord
- Cosmetic blush and cotton-tip swab
- Fabric glue
- Polyester fiberfill
- Large-eye embroidery needle
- Basic sewing supplies and equipment

Assembly
If making a quantity of ornaments, sew long strips of fabric together and subcut into 10-inch-long segments.

Stitch right sides together using a ¼-inch seam allowance unless otherwise indicated.

Use patterns provided on insert. Transfer all markings to fabric.

Santa & Angel Ornaments
Angel With Bell
Placement Diagram 6½" high

Santa & Angel Ornaments
Santa Ornament
Placement Diagram 4" x 5¼"

1. Cut one each 2 x 10-inch A strip pale pink solid, 2½ x 10-inch B strip of one red-and-white print and 3 x 10-inch C strip of second red-and-white print.

2. Join strips together in alphabetical order; press seams in one direction.

3. Place Santa pattern on wrong side of the A-B-C strip set, matching lines on pattern with seams on the strip, and trace.

4. Fold strip right sides together, carefully matching seam lines; pin to hold.

5. Sew all around on marked line, leaving an opening at one side as marked on pattern.

6. Cut out ¼ inch from seam; clip curves, turn right side out and stuff firmly with fiberfill. Fold in seam allowance at opening; hand-stitch closed.

7. Draw beard and mustache patterns on wrong side of white tonal. Fold fabric in half right sides together with drawn pattern on top; pin to batting scrap.

8. Stitch all around on marked lines; cut out ⅛ inch from seam; clip curves and indents. Trim batting very close to seam on mustache.

9. Cut a slash through one layer only on each piece as indicated on patterns. Turn right side out through openings; press. Hand-stitch openings closed.

10. Hand-quilt around beard about ¼ inch from edge with white quilting thread. Hand-stitch gathering stitches down the center of the mustache with matching thread; pull tight to gather and wrap thread around center twice before knotting.

11. Sew black buttons to face for eyes and 6mm red bead for nose. Apply glue to back of beard at top and center, leaving sides free; press in place on face. Glue mustache to top of beard directly below nose.

12. Glue ⅜-inch-wide black velvet ribbon over body seam, butting ends together at center front. Glue red star button over ends.

13. Wrap holly garland around top of head to shape; remove and twist ends together. Place on head twisted ends in back; tack in place.

14. Sew three small red E beads to garland at one side.

15. For hanger, thread large-eye embroidery needle with red cord; take a small stitch at top back of head. Remove cord from needle; tie ends in knot. Clip ends close to knot to finish. ■

Santa Gift-Card Holders

Designs by Chris Malone

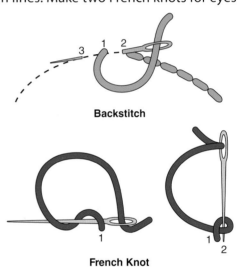

Finished Sizes

Santa Moon: 4 x 4 inches
Santa Face: 3½ x 4¾ inches

Materials

- Small piece each red-with-white and white-with-red prints
- 1 (8-inch) square white solid
- Small piece batting
- 8 inches ¼-inch-wide red ribbon
- 4 (½-inch-diameter) white buttons
- Coordinating red standard embroidery floss
- Transfer pen (air- or water-soluble)
- Small piece of toweling
- Embroidery needle
- 5- or 6-inch embroidery hoop
- Basic sewing tools and equipment

Project Note

Materials listed will make one of the gift-card holders. Cutting and Assembly instructions are for both gift-card holders.

Cutting

For Santa Moon:

From red-with-white print:
- Cut 2 each 1 x 3½-inch Santa Moon side border strips and 1 x 4½-inch Santa Moon top/bottom border strips.
- Cut 1 (4½-inch) square for Santa Moon backing.

For Santa Face:

From red-with-white print:
- Cut 2 each 1 x 4¼-inch Santa Face side border strips and 1 x 5¼-inch top/bottom border strips.
- Cut 1 (4 x 5¼-inch) rectangle for Santa Face backing.

For Santa Moon or Santa Face:

From white-with-red print:
- Cut 1 each 4½ x 7-inch and 4 x 7-inch pockets.

From batting:
- Cut 1 each 4½-inch square and 4 x 5¼-inch rectangle.

Assembly

Stitch right sides together using a ¼-inch seam allowance. Use embroidery diagrams provided on insert. Use two strands of embroidery floss for all embroidery.

1. Transfer embroidery pattern to center of white fabric. Place fabric in hoop.

2. For Santa Moon, work a backstitch over all pattern lines. Make two French knots for eyes.

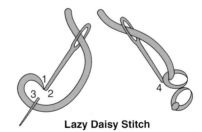

Backstitch

French Knot

3. For Santa Face, work a backstitch over pattern lines. Make two French knots for eyes. At each dot on the border pattern, make two Lazy daisy stitches, one slanting inward and one slanting outward (Figure 1). Make a French knot at the base of the Lazy daisy stitches and a small straight stitch between the motifs.

Lazy daisy

French knot

Figure 1

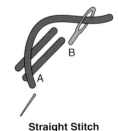

Lazy Daisy Stitch

Straight Stitch

4. Remove from hoop and remove any marking lines. Lay embroidery right side down on terry towel and press.

5. With embroidery centered, trim Santa Moon to 3½ inches square or Santa Face to 3 x 4¼ inches.

6. Choosing appropriate border strips, stitch side border strips and then top and bottom border strips to embroidered piece (Figure 2); press seams toward borders.

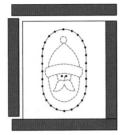

Figure 2

7. Fold and press pocket in half lengthwise wrong sides together. Santa Moon pocket will measure 4½ x 3½ inches and Santa Face 4 x 3½ inches.

8. Place the pocket on the right side of the appropriate backing fabric with the raw edges matching at the bottom and sides (Figure 3). Position a hanging loop at top center of each back referring again to Figure 3.

Figure 3

9. Layer backing, pocket side up, batting and embroidered front, right side down, matching bottom edges (Figure 4).

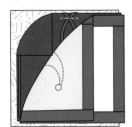

Figure 4

10. Stitch all around, leaving a 2½-inch opening at top. Trim batting close to seam, clip corners and turn right side out.

11. Fold opening seam allowance to inside. Fold the ribbon in half and insert ends ½ inch into opening; pin. Hand-stitch opening closed, catching ribbon in stitches.

12. Stitch a button to each corner of the front of the ornament to finish. Use the pocket in the back for a gift card or small gifts. ∎

Nativity Ornaments

Designs by Kate Laucomer

Finished Sizes
Large ovals: 6⅛ x 6¾ inches
Small ovals: 4⅝ x 6½ inches

Materials
- Wide variety scraps for appliqué
- ½ yard tan for background
- ½ yard red woven check for backing
- ½ yard white felt
- Scraps fusible web
- Black 6-strand embroidery floss
- Pinking shears or rotary cutter with pinking blade
- 2 yards twine or narrow ribbon for hangers
- Basic sewing supplies and equipment

Project Note
Instructions are for one large oval with Mary, Joseph and Baby Jesus and two small ovals showing Joseph on one and Mary and Baby Jesus on the other.

Assembly
1. Trace ovals on tan background fabric as directed on templates provided on insert. Cut out at least ½ inch larger on all sides.

2. Trace appliqué shapes on paper side of fusible web as directed on templates provided on insert. Fuse to fabrics as directed by manufacturer. Cut out and arrange within tan ovals, referring to Placement Diagrams. Fuse in place. With two strands of embroidery floss, work buttonhole stitch around edges.

3. With pinking shears or rotary cutter, cut around marked oval shapes.

4. Place white felt on work surface. With chalk or washout marker, draw a line ¼ inch around outside of each tan oval. Cut out with pinking shears or rotary cutter.

5. Place red woven check fabric on work surface right side up. With chalk or washout marker, draw a line ¼ inch around outside of each white felt oval. Cut out with pinking shears or rotary cutter.

6. Cut 9-inch lengths of twine or ribbon for hangers. Twine may be untwisted for thinner pieces and it may be pressed for easier handling.

7. Cut a 1-inch square of fusible web. Fuse it to the inside of backing fabric in correct position for hanging referring to samples. Remove paper. Position cut ends of twine or ribbon on webbing square. Position felt oval over backing and press from back to fuse hanger in place. Repeat for each ornament.

8. Center each appliquéd oval over appropriate felt/backing ovals. Stitch around edges with 6 strands of black embroidery floss using a primitive quilting stitch to finish.

Alternative Traditional Binding
1. Follow steps 1 and 2 above. Cut out ovals with regular scissors or rotary cutter.

2. Cut felt and backing same size for each ornament.

3. Purchase or make 4 yards bias binding. Layer backing, felt and appliquéd ornament and bind to finish. Stitch loop of twine or ribbon to backing for hanging. ■

Nativity Ornaments
Mary, Joseph and Baby Jesus
Placement Diagram approximately 6$\frac{1}{8}$" x 6$\frac{3}{4}$"

Nativity Ornaments
Mary and Baby Jesus
Placement Diagram approximately 4$\frac{5}{8}$" x 6$\frac{1}{2}$"

Nativity Ornaments
Joseph
Placement Diagram approximately 4$\frac{5}{8}$" x 6$\frac{1}{2}$"

Nativity Ornaments
Camel
Placement Diagram approximately 6$\frac{3}{4}$" x 6$\frac{1}{8}$"

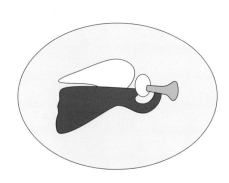

Nativity Ornaments
Angel
Placement Diagram approximately 6$\frac{1}{2}$" x 4$\frac{5}{8}$"

Nativity Ornaments
Donkey
Placement Diagram approximately 6$\frac{1}{2}$" x 4$\frac{5}{8}$"

Nativity Ornaments
Wise Man
Placement Diagram approximately 4$\frac{5}{8}$" x 6$\frac{1}{2}$"

Nativity Ornaments
Shepherd
Placement Diagram approximately 4$\frac{5}{8}$" x 6$\frac{1}{2}$"

Gingerbread Cheer

Design by Diane Bunker

Finished Size
4 x 4½ inches

Materials
- 6 x 10-inch tan or light brown print
- ½ yard ¼-inch-wide red ribbon
- Polyester fiberfill
- Coordinating thread
- Acrylic paint white, red and black
- White dimensional paint
- Variety paintbrushes
- Black permanent marker with fine and ultrafine tips
- 3 small flat back red crystals
- Craft glue
- Wire hanger
- Basic sewing supplies and equipment

Assembly
Use pattern provided on insert. Transfer all marks to fabric. Stitch right sides together using a ⅛-inch seam allowance.

1. Cut two bodies from tan or light brown print.

2. Paint face using black for eyes, eyebrows and mouth; watered-down red for cheeks and white for eye twinkle. Let dry.

3. Stitch front and back together leaving opening between circles for turning. Clip curves and neck pivot; turn right side out and press.

4. Tightly stuff with fiberfill. Hand-stitch opening closed.

5. Apply red crystals to center of body where marked with glue or following manufacturer's instructions.

6. Paint rickrack trim around gingerbread man and bands on arms and legs with dimensional paint referring to the pattern and photo; let dry.

7. Tie ribbon around neck in a bow, and add a wire hanger to back. ■

Painting Tip
To make a smaller tip on your dimensional paint tube or bottle, wrap tape around the top rolling it between your fingers (Figure A).

Figure A

Primitive Angel

Design by Lynn Weglarz

Finished Size
4¼ x 3½ inches

Materials
Materials listed make 4 angels.

- ⅛ yard print fabric
- ⅛ yard tan fabric
- 1 package tan extra-wide double-fold bias tape
- Ribbon:
    1⅓ yards ⅜-inch-wide ribbon
    1⅓ yards 1½-inch-wide ribbon
- 1⅛ yards ⅛–¼-inch-wide ribbon
- 12 black size 3/0 sew-on snaps
- 4 small bells
- Fiberfill
- Black extra-fine permanent marking pen
- Powder blush with brush (or cotton swab)
- Basic sewing supplies and equipment

Cutting
Use patterns provided on insert. Transfer all marks to fabric. Cutting instructions are for 4 angels.

From print:
- Cut 8 Body pieces.

From tan:
- Cut 8 Head pieces.

From purchased bias tape:
- Cut one piece of bias tape 52 inches.

From ribbon:
- Cut 4 (12-inch) pieces of ⅜-inch-wide ribbon for neck bow.
- Cut 4 (12-inch) pieces of 1½-inch-wide ribbon for wings.
- Cut 4 (10-inch) pieces of ⅛–¼-inch-wide ribbon for hanger.

Assembly
Stitch right sides together using a ¼-inch seam allowance.

1. Edgestitch outer folded edges of bias tape together. Cut bias tape into eight 4-inch pieces for legs and four 5-inch pieces for arms; set aside.

2. Make a knot close to one end on all 4-inch leg pieces. Make a knot in the center of the 5-inch arm pieces.

3. To make one Primitive Angel, choose two each heads, bodies and legs and one arm.

4. Stitch heads together leaving bottom straight edge open. Turn right side out. Stuff head firmly with fiberfill.

5. Position legs on right side of wide bottom edge of one body at placement squares with knots toward narrow end (Figure 1); baste.

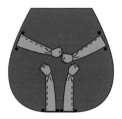

Figure 1

6. Position one arm on right side of body at place-ment squares with knot at center referring again to Figure 1; baste.

7. Position another body, right sides together with body/legs/arms unit. Stitch around edges keeping top edge open. Turn right side out and softly stuff body with fiberfill.

8. Finger-press top raw edge of body ¼ inch to wrong side. Hand-stitch close to fold around top edge with knotted thread (Figure 2a).

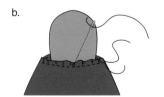

Figure 2

9. Insert head into opening, matching seams. Lightly pull stitching, gathering body close to head (Figure 2b). Secure head to body with several hand stitches.

10. Open snaps. Hand-stitch male half of six snaps to head, center snaps over seam. Draw eyes and freckles on face, if desired, using black pen.

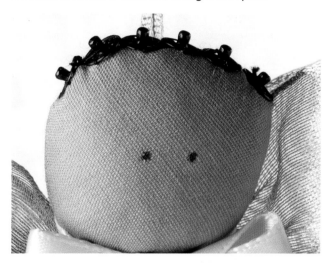

11. Tie ⅜-inch-wide ribbon around neck in a bow; trim ends as desired.

12. Overlap ends of a piece of 1½-inch ribbon at center about ½ inch forming two loops. Stitch through the center to secure.

13. Wrap thread around center several times pinching ribbon together to form wings; secure thread. Stitch wings to back of ornament (Figure 3).

Figure 3

14. Make a loop from 10-inch ribbon to form hanger. Hand-stitch ends of ribbon to back of head.

15. Stitch small bell to arm center knot.

16. Add powder blush to cheeks with brush or cotton swab.

17. Repeat steps 3–16 for remaining ornaments. ■

Angel in Lace

Design by Diane Bunker

Finished Size
3½ x 5½ inches

Materials
- 1 (9 x 12-inch) sheet beige felt
- 2 (2 x 3-inch) pieces sheer lace
- Red ribbon: 3 different (¾ x 6-inch) and 1 (1½ x 12-inch)
- 1 yard 1-inch-wide beige lace tipped with gold
- 1¾ x 18-inch piece beige lace tipped with gold
- 6 inches narrow ornate trim (optional)
- 26 gauge gold wire
- Wire cutters and round-nose pliers
- 2 beige pipe cleaners
- Polyester fiberfill
- Thread: brown, beige and red
- Fabric paints: red and yellow
- Variety paintbrushes
- Craft glue (optional)
- Wire hanger
- Basic sewing supplies and equipment

Preparation & Cutting
Use patterns provided on insert. Transfer all markings to fabric.

1. From beige felt, trace and cut front A and back B.

2. Free motion machine-straight stitch hair and nose with brown thread, eyes with black and mouth with red.

3. Rouge cheeks with watered-down red paint.

4. Paint about ½ inch of ends of one pipe cleaner red for shoes; let dry.

Assembly
Stitch right sides together using a ⅛-inch seam allowance.

1. Stitch the dress area of A and B together leaving the head and bottom of dress open.

2. Turn right side out, gently pulling head out through opening. Stitch head together with brown thread close to edges.

3. Lightly stuff head. Keep most of the stuffing in face area and stitch around the face area with brown thread.

4. Layer ribbons over laces and hand-gather stitch. Position widest ribbon/lace around dress bottom gathering to fit; hand-stitch in place.

5. Continue to add overlapping rows of ribbon/lace; gathering to fit and hand-stitching in place to cover the dress. *Note: Sample has five ribbon/lace layers. Sample also uses narrow ornate trim at bottom of dress.*

6. Gather stitch along the 3-inch edges of the sheer lace pieces (Figure 1a). Fold in half and stitch the 2-inch edges together (Figure 1b). Turn right side out to make two sleeves.

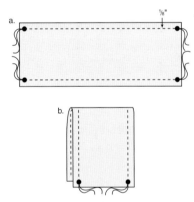

Figure 1

7. Place a sleeve approximately ½ inch from each end of the unpainted pipe cleaner. Gather each end of the sleeve tightly around the pipe cleaner at shoulders and wrists.

8. Hand-stitch to the back of the dress referring to Figure 2. Bend the arms to the front and wrap the hands together referring to the photo.

Figure 2

9. Bend the painted pipe cleaner into legs referring to Figure 3; insert them into the dress and hand-tack or glue in place.

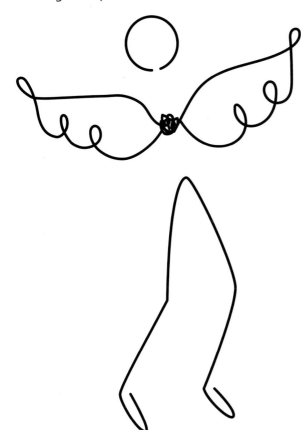

Figure 3

10. Bend the wire into the wing pattern beginning and ending at the center referring again to Figure 3. Wrap around the center and cut with wire cutters. Attach on top of the arms on the back.

11. Bend a 1½–2-inch piece of wire into an open circle as shown in Figure 3. Insert into the back of angel's head.

12. Add a wire hanger. ■

Poinsettia Perfection

Design by Linda Turner Griepentrog

Assembly

1. Follow sewing machine manual instructions to set your machine for free-motion stitching. Thread machine with metallic thread in the needle and thread to match felt in bobbin.

2. Free-motion stitch veins in each leaf referring to Figure 2.

Figure 2

3. Carefully cut out each petal just inside the drawn lines and stack by size.

4. Starting on the outer edge, space five large petals around the backing circle and hand-stitch the tips to the circle center (Figure 3).

Figure 3

Figure 4

5. Add a second layer of large petals, spacing them between the first petals. Hand-stitch the tips to the circle center (Figure 4).

6. Top the large petals with five small petals. Adjust petals as needed to form a full blossom. Hand-stitch the tips to the circle center.

7. Fold the silver cord in half and knot the ends together. Place the knotted ends between the backing circle and the petals; hand-stitch in place to form a hanging loop.

8. Stitch the button in the center of the petals, covering the tips and referring to the photo. ∎

Finished Size
Approximately 6 inches

Materials
- 1 (9 x 12-inch) rectangle glitter felt
- 1/3 yard small silver cord
- 1-inch-diameter rhinestone button
- Silver metallic machine embroidery thread
- Basic sewing supplies and equipment

Cutting
Use patterns provided on insert. Transfer all markings to fabric.

From felt:
- Cut 1 (1¼-inch) circle for backing.
- Trace 9 large and 5 small petals onto felt leaving at least ¼ inch between. Do not cut apart (Figure 1).

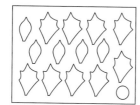

Figure 1

Christmas Tussie Mussie

Design by Chris Malone

Finished Size
4½ x 6½ (not including hanger and tassel)

Materials
- 1 (6½-inch) square each two coordinating metallic gold fabrics
- 6½-inch square thin batting
- 3-inch-long metallic gold tassel
- ¾-inch-diameter gold button
- 20 inches of ⅜-inch-wide metallic gold wire-edge ribbon
- Basic sewing tools and equipment

Assembly
Stitch right sides together using a ¼-inch seam allowance.

1. Layer fabric squares right sides together on batting; pin. Stitch all around leaving a 3-inch opening on one side. Trim corners and batting close to seam. Turn right side out; press.

2. Fold opening seam allowance to inside and hand-stitch opening closed.

3. Choose a lining side then position the tassel at one corner with fringe hanging down. Tack top end of tassel to fabric to secure (Figure 1).

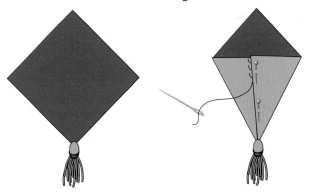

Figure 1   **Figure 2**

4. Fold corners to center overlapping ½ inch; pin. Bring edges together at bottom tasseled point; pin. Hand-stitch edges together from top to bottom of edge (Figure 2).

5. Fold remaining corner down to expose the lining as shown in photo. Stitch the gold button at the corner to hold.

6. To make a hanger, fold ribbon in half. Hand-stitch ribbon together 4 inches down from loop. Pull thread, gathering tightly, and knot but do not clip the thread (Figure 3).

7. Tie ribbon ends in a bow. Use thread ends to tack bow center to the top back of the cone for a hanger; trim ribbon ends. ■

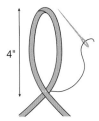

4"

Figure 3

Ribbons & Taffeta

Design by Chris Malone

Finished Size
3 inches in diameter

Materials
• 3-inch-diameter plastic foam ball
• 1 (10-inch) square red moiré, taffeta, satin or similar specialty fabric
• Ribbon:
    9 inches 1½-inch-wide green
    ½ yard ⅜-inch-wide gold wire-edged
    1 yard ⅞-inch-wide gold wire-edged
• 10 inches gold cord
• 2 long straight pins
• Hot-glue gun or quick-drying fabric adhesive
• Craft scissors
• Basic sewing tools and equipment

Assembly
1. Cut a 10-inch-diameter circle from red fabric.

2. Finger-press a ³⁄₁₆-inch hem around edge of the fabric circle as you sew gathering stitches close to the fold with a knotted double strand of red thread around circle (Figure 1).

Figure 1

3. Place ball in center of wrong side of fabric and pull thread to bring fabric up and cover the ball. Knot and clip thread (Figure 2).

Figure 2

4. To make a hanger, fold gold cord in half and tie a knot near the ends. Place knot in hole where gathers come together at top of the ball. Insert two long pins through cord and into ball to secure hanger cord (Figure 3).

Figure 3

5. To make leaves, cut green ribbon into three 3-inch-long pieces. Fold ends toward center of each piece (Figure 4).

Figure 4

6. Using a double strand of matching thread, hand-gather stitch across the straight bottom edge through all layers referring to Figure 5.

Figure 5

7. Pull thread gathering ribbon tightly. Wrap thread around the leaf base several times and knot (Figure 6). Repeat to make a total of three leaves.

Figure 6

8. Glue the leaves evenly around the cord knot at the top of the ball.

9. To make ribbon roses, cut the ⅞-inch-wide gold wire-edged ribbon into three 12-inch pieces. Tie a knot near the end of one ribbon. At the opposite end, pull the wire from the casing along one edge sliding ribbon along wire to tightly gather entire length (Figure 7). Do not cut wire.

Figure 7

10. Hold ribbon knot between thumb and forefinger of one hand, use other hand to wrap gathered ribbon around the knot several times. Fold the raw edge of ribbon under and wrap wire tightly around knotted base (Figure 8). Trim excess wire; flatten and crimp ribbon edges.

Figure 8

11. Repeat steps 9 and 10 to make a total of three roses.

12. Apply glue to the base of each rose and press to ball top, between leaves and around the hanging cord.

13. Tie ⅜-inch-wide ribbon into a bow. Apply glue to the knotted center and press down into the center of rose embellishment. Trim the ends as desired and use your fingers to arrange the bow loops and tails. ∎

Lollipop, Lollipop

Design by Linda Turner Griepentrog

Finished Size
7 inches long, 3-inch diameter (excluding hanger)

Materials
- 1 yard white premade piping
- 1⅛ yards red premade piping
- 3-inch-diameter circle white felt
- ⅓ yard ⅜-inch-wide grosgrain ribbon
- ⅓ yard nylon thread or clear fishing line
- 1 (4-inch-wide) cellophane food bag
- 1 (6-inch) lollipop stick
- Fabric glue
- Fabric clamps
- Basic sewing tools and equipment

Assembly

1. Lay the red and white piping together with the red extending about 2 inches at each end (Figure 1).

Figure 1   **Figure 2**

2. Beginning at one end, coil the red piping tightly to form the lollipop center. Hand-stitch in place from the underside (Figure 2).

3. Tuck under the white end as you roll, and continue rolling and hand stitching together for the length of the piping. Tuck the outer white end under and continue to wrap the red until the piping ends, tucking under the end. Be sure the circle is stitched enough to secure the shape (Figure 3).

Figure 3   **Figure 4**

4. Glue the felt circle to the coiled lollipop underside, sandwiching the end of the stick between the layers (Figure 4). Clamp in place to dry.

5. Cut the cellophane bag 5 inches long and cut a small slit in the upper edge.

6. When the lollipop is thoroughly dry, hand stitch a nylon thread or fishing line hanger loop in the upper edge; knot the ends together.

7. Insert the lollipop into the bag and thread the hanger loop through the bag slit. Tie the bag with a ribbon bow to secure it around the lollipop. ■

Holiday Sentiments

Designs by Margie Ullery

Finished Size
6 x 6 inches

Materials
- 7-inch square each red, white and green wool
- 3 (7-inch) squares print
- Polyester fiberfill
- Metallic embroidery floss: red, gold and silver
- Embroidery needle
- 12 inches each gold, silver and red ¼-inch-wide ribbon
- Pinking shears
- Decorative-edge rotary cutter (optional)
- Basic sewing supplies and equipment

Assembly
1. Transfer embroidery design provided on insert to center of each wool square.

2. Using 3 strands of floss, stitch words in stem stitch and stars in straight stitch referring to photo.

3. Layer and pin a wool and print square wrong sides together matching edges. With design centered, trim to 6 inches square with a decorative rotary cutter or pinking shears.

4. Machine-stitch around square ¼ inch from edges, leave a 2½-inch opening on one side. Stuff to desired fullness and stitch opening closed.

5. Knot ends of ribbon and hand-stitch in place at top corners of square for hanger.

6. Repeat steps 4 and 5 to complete all three ornaments. ■

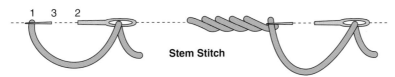

Stem Stitch

Patchwork Star

Design by Chris Malone

Finished Size
6 x 6 inches

Materials
- 1 (4½ x 3½-inch) scrap each five red-with-white prints
- 1 (7-inch) square red print
- 1 (2½-inch) square white-with-red print
- Buttons:
    1 (⅞-inch-diameter) cover button kit
    1 any size two-holed flat white
- Button thread
- 20 inches of ⅜-inch-wide red with white dots ribbon
- Fiberfill stuffing
- Basic sewing tools and equipment

Assembly

Use pattern provided on insert. Cut shapes accurately and use a consistent seam allowance. Stitch seams ¼ inch wide right sides together.

1. Cut one diamond shape from each of the red-with-white prints.

2. Stitch two diamond shapes together on one side; stop stitching ¼ inch from the end of the seam (Figure 1); backstitch to secure and press seam open (Figure 2).

Figure 1

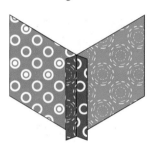

Figure 2

3. Add a third diamond in the same manner.

4. Stitch remaining two diamonds together referring to step 2 to make two units as shown in Figure 3.

Figure 3

5. Join the two units stitching the remaining seams individually from the outside point to the center, again stopping ¼ inch from the end. Press seams open.

6. Pin pieced star to the red print square, right sides together; stitch all around, leaving an opening on one side (Figure 4).

Figure 4

7. Trim red print square to match pieced star. Trim points at an angle. Turn right side out through the opening, gently pushing out points.

8. Stuff the star with fiberfill to a medium firmness. Fold in the seam allowance on the opening and slip stitch the opening closed.

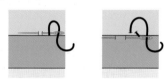

Slip Stitch

9. Follow manufacturer's directions to cover button with white-with-red fabric.

10. Using two strands of button thread, sew the covered button to the pieced star center all the way through to the center back. Add the white button to the back and pull to indent slightly. Stitch through the buttons several times; knot and clip the thread.

11. To make hanger, fold ribbon in half. Using red thread, stitch through ribbon 3 inches down from the loop (Figure 5). Knot, but do not clip, the thread. Tie ribbon ends into a small bow. Tack the bow and hanging loop to the top of the bird as shown in the photo. ■

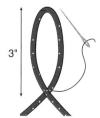

3"

Figure 5

Beaded Patchwork

Designs by Chris Malone

Finished Size
Ball Ornament: 5¼ x 6⅛ inches, excluding
   ribbon and beads
Bell Ornament: 5 x 5⅛ inches, excluding
   ribbon and beads

Materials
- Materials listed are for both Ball and Bell
  Ornaments.
- 5–7 white-with-gold holiday print scraps
- 2 x 3-inch gold metallic scrap
- 3 (7-inch) squares and scraps batting
- All-purpose thread to match fabrics
- Quilting thread
- Scrap 1-inch-wide red/gold metallic ribbon
- 3 (24-inch) lengths ⅜-inch-wide red
  wire-edge ribbon
- Assortment of coordinating 3–10mm glass beads
- Beeswax
- Basic sewing supplies and equipment

Ball Ornament

Cutting
Use patterns provided on insert. Transfer all
markings to fabric.

From white-with-gold holiday print scraps:
- Cut 1 each (1½–2-inch x 6-inch) strips.
- Cut 1 (6-inch) square.

From gold metallic scrap:
- Cut 2 Ball Caps, reverse 1.

Completing Ball Ornament
Stitch right sides together using a ¼-inch seam
allowance unless otherwise indicated.

Use patterns provided on insert. Transfer all
markings to fabric.

1. Join the strips along the 6-inch
length to make a rectangle as
shown in Figure 1; press seams
in one direction.

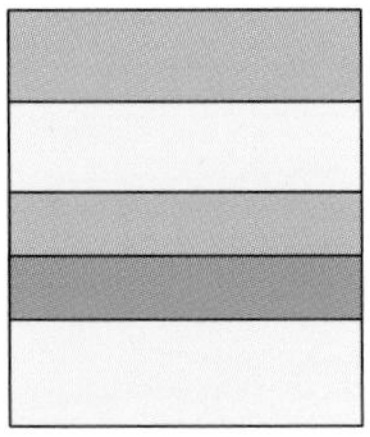

Figure 1

2. Trace the Ball Ornament pattern onto the wrong
side of the 6-inch square.

3. Layer and pin marked square, marked side up;
pieced rectangle, right side up, and 7-inch
square batting.

4. Stitch all around on traced lines, leaving opening
at top as marked on pattern. Cut out; trim batting
close to seam and clip curves. Turn right side out
and press flat.

5. Layer Ball Cap pieces right sides together on
scrap of batting; repeat step 4 leaving bottom open.

6. Insert Ball Cap into opening in top of ball, fold
opening seam to inside and hand-stitch closed,
catching cap in stitches.

7. Machine-stitch in the ditch of seams.

8. Hand-stitch glass beads across second band of
ball ornament. *Note: The sample has five sets of three
beads each with a ¼-inch space between sets.*

9. Anchor a doubled thread at the bottom tip of
the ornament; string on about three larger glass
beads and then a smaller bead at the end, making
a 1¾-inch dangle.

10. Skipping the last bead on the string, insert the
needle back through the other beads and into the
fabric. Adjust the tension of the dangle by holding
onto the last bead while pulling on the thread; knot
and clip the thread.

11. Fold one 24-inch length of ribbon in half and tie
a knot about 4 inches from the end of the loop. Tie
the free ends in a bow.

12. Tack the ribbon hanger to the top back of the
ornament. Trim the ends as needed; tie a knot at
each end.

Bell Ornament

Cutting

From white-with-gold holiday print scraps:
- Cut 1 each (1½–2-inch x 6-inch) strips.
- Cut 1 (6-inch) square.

Completing Bell Ornament

Stitch right sides together using a ¼-inch seam allowance unless otherwise indicated.

Use patterns provided on insert. Transfer all markings to fabric.

1. Repeat steps 1–4 of Completing Ball Ornament to complete the bell ornament, referring to Figure 2. Hand-stitch the bottom opening closed after turning.

Figure 2

2. Hand-sew glass beads across the second band of the bell ornament. *Note: The model has two red beads alternating with single gold beads placed about ³⁄₁₆ inch between sets.*

3. Referring to steps 9 and 10 of Completing Ball Ornament make a 1½-inch dangle.

4. Repeat steps 11 and 12 of Completing Ball Ornament to make ribbon hanger. ∎

Beaded Patchwork
Ball Ornament Placement Diagram 5¼" x 6⅛",
excluding ribbon and beads

Beaded Patchwork
Bell Ornament Placement Diagram 5" x 5⅛",
excluding ribbon and beads

Candy Cane Stocking

Design by Margie Ullery

Finished Size
4½ x 5 inches

Materials
- 3½-inch square solid white
- 6-inch square red stripe
- 6-inch square solid red
- 3-inch square paper backed fusible web
- Thread to match
- 8 inches craft white fur trim
- 10 inches ⅛-inch-wide white ribbon
- Polyester fiberfill
- Basic sewing supplies and equipment

Cutting
Use pattern provided on insert. Transfer all markings to fabric.

From solid white:
- Fuse fusible web to wrong side of solid white. Trace and cut 1 each toe and heel. Do not remove paper.

From red stripe:
- Cut 1 stocking for front.

From solid red:
- Cut 1 stocking for back.

Assembly
Stitch right sides together using a ⅛-inch seam allowance.

1. Remove paper from toe and heel and fuse in place to stocking front. Machine-blanket stitch around inner edges of toe and heel referring to photo.

2. Stitch front and back stocking together; leave top of stocking open. Clip curves and turn right side out; press flat.

3. Stuff with fiberfill to desired fullness.

4. Fold ribbon in half and position and pin in stocking corner. Hand-stitch stocking top closed.

5. Pin and hand-stitch fur trim around stocking top referring to photo. ■

Weiner Wonderland

Design by Chris Malone

Finished Size
4½ x 3½ inches

Materials
- Small piece red-with-white print
- 8-inch square white solid
- 5 x 4-inch piece batting
- 18 inches ⅜-inch-wide red sheer ribbon
- Standard embroidery floss: red and white
- Transfer pen (air- or water-soluble)
- Embroidery needle
- 4- or 5-inch embroidery hoop
- Small piece of toweling
- Basic sewing tools and equipment

Cutting

From red-with-white print:
- Cut 2 each 1 x 3-inch side border strips and 1 x 5-inch top/bottom border strips.
- Cut 1 (5 x 4-inch) backing.

Assembly
Stitch right sides together using ¼-inch seam allowance. Use embroidery diagram provided on insert. Use two strands of floss for all embroidery.

1. Transfer embroidery pattern to center of white fabric. Place fabric in hoop.

2. For embroidery, stitch backstitch over all pattern lines and a French knot for the nose and eye using red floss. Stitch French knot snowflakes in white floss. Refer to page 16 for embroidery stitch diagrams and Figure 1 below for placement.

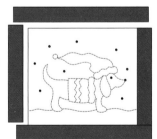

Figure 1

3. Remove from hoop and remove any marking lines. Lay embroidery right side down on terry towel and press.

4. With embroidery centered, trim fabric to 4 x 3 inches.

5. Stitch side border strips and then top and bottom border strips to embroidered piece (Figure 1); press seams toward borders.

6. Layer and pin embroidered front, right side up; back, right side down; and batting. Stitch all around, leaving a 2½-inch opening at top. Trim batting close to seam, clip corners and turn right side out.

7. Fold opening seam allowance to inside and hand-stitch opening closed.

8. Machine-stitch between the borders and the embroidered center, right at the seam line.

9. To make a hanger, fold ribbon in half. Hand-stitch ribbon together 3 inches down from loop. Pull thread, gathering tightly, and knot but do not clip the thread (Figure 2).

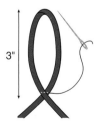

3"

Figure 2

10. Tie ribbon ends in a bow. Use thread ends to tack bow center to the top of ornament; trim ribbon ends. ■

Little Rudolf

Design by Tie Dye Diva Patterns

Finished Size
Approximately 3½-inch diameter

Materials
- Scraps black, pink, red, brown felt or polyester fleece
- 3-inch square pink polyester fleece
- ¼ yard tan polyester fleece
- Black and white embroidery thread
- Embroidery needle
- Polyester fiberfill
- 5-inch piece of ¼–½-inch-wide ribbon or rickrack
- Basic sewing supplies and equipment

Cutting
Use patterns provided on insert. Transfer all markings to fabric.

From felt or polyester fleece:
- Cut 2 each: outer ears, tan fleece; inner ears, pink fleece; eyes, black fleece or felt; cheeks, pink fleece or felt; antlers, brown felt.
- Cut 1 each: nose, red fleece or felt.

From tan fleece:
- Cut 6 head panels.
  Cut with fabric stretch as marked.

Assembly
Stitch right sides together using a ⅛-inch seam allowance unless otherwise indicated.

1. Stitch two head panels together referring to Figure 1a. Finger-press the seam open and stitch a third panel to the unit referring to Figure 1b creating the back unit of the ornament; set aside.

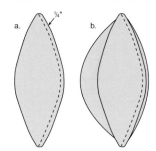

Figure 1

2. Stitch two remaining head panels together to make the face unit referring again to Figure 1a.

3. Hand-sew the eyes, cheeks and nose to the face unit centering on the seam (Figure 2). Embroider the mouth using black thread referring to the photo and Figure 2. Add embroidered eye highlights with white embroidery thread.

Figure 2

4. Stitch an outer and inner ear together leaving the bottom straight edge open; turn right side out.

5. Fold a pleat at bottom edge of ear pink sides together; hand-baste in place.

6. Referring to Figure 3, position the antlers and ears with straight edges aligned with top side edges of face unit; baste.

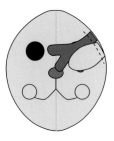

Figure 3

7. Fold ribbon or rickrack in half and baste in place at top of face unit for loop.

8. Stitch the remaining head panel to the face unit (Figure 4).

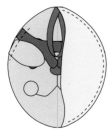

Figure 4

9. Stitch the back and face units together leaving a 2-inch opening for turning and stuffing in one seam.

10. Turn right side out, stuff as desired and hand-stitch opening closed. ■

Perky Penguin

Design by Diane Bunker

Finished Size
2½ x 6 inches

Materials
- Small scrap orange felt
- 1 (3 x 5-inch) piece white tonal
- 1 fat quarter white tonal with dots
- Cotton batting
- Black, red and orange thread
- Paper-backed fusible web
- Thrift store red sweater
- Red acrylic yarn
- 24 inches ¼-inch-wide red ribbon
- 2 inches ¼-inch-wide black elastic
- Scrap Christmas wrapping paper
- Scrap plastic foam sheet
- Candy cane
- Fiberfill stuffing
- Small variety of red seed beads
- Fabric glue
- Fine and ultrafine black markers
- Fabric paints: white, red, black
- Variety paintbrushes
- Glossy accents glaze (optional)
- Twinkles Crystal Glitter (optional)
- Basic sewing supplies and equipment

Preparation & Cutting
Use patterns provided on insert. Transfer all markings to fabric.

From orange felt:
- Trace 1 beak G and 2 feet H; stitch detail lines on feet with orange thread.
  Cut out beak and feet.

From white tonal:
- Trace front C on paper side of fusible web with the ultrafine marker. Fuse to wrong side of fabric. Paint eyes and rouge checks using watered-down red as shown in photo.
  Cut out C when dry.

From white tonal with dots:
- Lightly paint with black and large brush to stain fabric. Let dry.
  Cut 1 each front A and B, back D, tail E and 4 wing F pieces.

From cotton batting:
- Cut 1 front A and 2 wing F pieces.

Assembly
1. Center and fuse front C to front A. Blanket-stitch with black thread around C.

2. Layer and pin front A batting; A, right side up; and front B, right side down at bottom edge of A. Stitch bottom seam referring to Figure 1. Clip curves and at end of stitching, turn and press. Stitch beak to face referring to sample and completing Penguin front.

Figure 1

3. Stitch back D and tail E in same manner (Figure 2). Clip at end of stitching and trim tail point at an angle; turn and press.

Figure 2   **Figure 3**

4. Cut two 1-inch pieces of black elastic. Fold and stitch with black thread to front tail section referring to Figure 3a.

5. Stitch feet over elastic referring to Figure 3b completing Penguin back.

6. Stitch front and back together leaving bottom open for turning; turn and press. Hand-stitch bottom closed with black thread.

7. Layer wing batting; wing, right side up; and wing, right side down. Stitch, leaving space open between squares for turning.

8. Turn right side out. Press opening seams to inside and hand-stitch closed.

9. Position and hand-stitch wings to front at neck with wing tips forward to hold gift (Figure 4).

Figure 4

10. To make gift, cut small cube from plastic foam sheet. Wrap with paper scraps and tie with red ribbon. Glue wing tips to opposite sides of gift.

11. To make hat, cut 2 x 4½-inch piece from thrift store sweater sleeve cuff. Stitch together making a tube. Stitch gathering stitch around cut edge and pull tight.

12. Turn hat right side out and roll up bottom to form hat cuff. Stuff lightly and stitch to Penguin head.

13. Make hat pompom by wrapping red yarn around 2 fingers 10 times. Carefully remove from fingers and tightly tie a piece of yarn at center. Fluff and trim pompom to even shape and stitch to top of hat.

14. Cut six pieces of yarn 18 inches long; divide into three 2-strand sections and braid. Tie off ends with red thread leaving a fringe on each to make scarf.

15. Wrap scarf around neck bringing one of the ends under the scarf. Stitch a variety of seed beads to the scarf and pompom.

16. If using glossy accents, add a drop to eyes after paint dries. This gives eye a rounded, glossy look. If desired, add dot of Twinkles Glitter to eye twinkle dot.

17. Add wire hanger and candy cane to back or through the elastic under the feet. ■

Tweetie Bird

Design by Chris Malone

Finished Size
About 7 x 4½ inches

Materials
- Small piece each red, green and gold tonals
- 2 (¼-inch-diameter) black buttons
- Tree branch approximately 6½ inches long (with a fork to support bird)
- 18 inches ⅜-inch-wide red transparent ribbon
- Small piece thin batting
- Seam sealant
- Quick-set fabric glue or hot-glue gun
- Basic sewing tools and equipment

Assembly
Use patterns provided on insert. Transfer all markings to fabric.

1. Leaving ½ inch between shapes, trace one body and two wings on wrong side of red, three leaves on wrong side of green and one beak on wrong side of gold.

2. Fold fabrics in half right sides together with marked shapes on top; pin to batting.

3. Stitch the beak on the marked lines, leaving open at the bottom edge. Cut out ⅛ inch from the seam and turn right side out; press.

4. Stitch all around body on marked line, leaving open between circles. Cut out ⅛ inch from the seam.

5. Insert pointed end of beak into opening, matching raw edges, and pin (Figure 1). Stitch opening closed catching beak in seam.

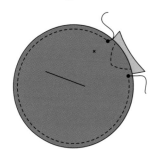

Figure 1

6. Cut a slash through one layer of fabric in stitched body. Apply seam sealant to slash edges and let dry. Turn bird right side out through slash opening and hand-stitch edges closed; press.

7. Stitch all around wings. Refer to step 6 to complete wings. If desired, quilt a wing shape on each wing with red thread.

8. Apply glue sparingly down the center of wing on slashed side. Glue wings to each side of body, covering body slash line.

9. Sew a black button on each side of the bird for eyes.

10. Stitch all around leaves. Refer to step 6 to complete leaves. If desired, quilt vein lines in each leaf.

11. To shape leaves, fold a small pleat into rounded end of each leaf. Secure fold with a few hand stitches at the edge (Figure 2).

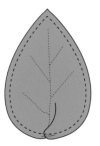

Figure 2

12. Arrange the bird and leaves on the branch. *Note: Positioning will vary from sample depending on branch shape. Use fork in branch to help support the bird.*

13. Lift each piece and apply glue where it touches the branch; press in place.

14. To make hanger, fold ribbon in half. Using red thread, stitch through ribbon 3 inches down from the loop. Knot, but do not clip, the thread (Figure 3). Tie ribbon ends into a small bow. Tack the bow and hanging loop to the top of the bird as shown in the photo. ∎

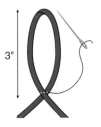

3"

Figure 3

Mouse in a Mitten

Design by Diane Bunker

Finished Size
3 x 6½ inches

Materials
- Small scrap white polyester fleece
- 1 (6 x 5-inch) rectangle red/white stripe
- 1 (8-inch) square gray polyester fleece
- 1 (8 x 5-inch) rectangle dark blue velvet
- Black and white all-purpose thread
- 5 inches white fur trim
- ¼ inch red ribbon
- 2 gray pipe cleaners
- Christmas greenery and holly berries
- Candy cane
- Fiberfill stuffing
- Craft glue
- Embroidery needle
- Fine and ultrafine black permanent markers
- Acrylic fabric paints: white, red, black
- Variety paintbrushes
- Glossy accents glaze (optional)
- Twinkles Crystal Glitter (optional)
- Basic sewing supplies and equipment

Preparation & Cutting
Use patterns provided on insert. Transfer all markings to fabric.

From white fleece:
- Cut 2 inner ear patterns.

From red/white stripe:
- Cut 1 (2½ x 5½-inch) shirt rectangle and 2 (2 x 3½-inch) sleeve rectangles.

From gray fleece:
- Trace 2 each body and ear and 4 arm patterns onto fleece; transfer face markings to 1 body. Free motion machine-straight stitch face features. Refer to machine manual for setup.
  Cut out patterns.

From dark blue velvet:
- Cut 2 mittens.

From white thread:
- Cut 24 inches and pass through a puddle of craft glue to stiffen. Let dry. **Note:** *If desired use glossy accents glaze instead of glue wherever glue is indicated.*

Assembly
Stitch right sides together using a ⅛-inch seam allowance unless otherwise indicated.

1. Cut two ¾-inch pieces of pipe cleaner. Make two pipe cleaner circles.

2. Stitch dart in ears (Figure 1). Position pipe cleaner circles between ear and inner ear; stitch inner ear to ear to secure.

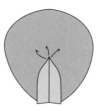

Figure 1

3. Pin ears at solid circles on head with inner ear toward face. Position bodies right sides together and stitch together leaving body bottom open. Clip at neck where marked and around head.

4. Stitch arms together leaving bottoms open; turn right side out.

5. Stitch mittens together leaving the top open. Clip seam at thumb and around curves; turn right side out.

6. Stuff the body and mitten with fiberfill stuffing. Do not stuff arms.

7. Stitch gathering stitch along one long edge of shirt and both long edges of sleeve pieces. Fold each in half matching short sides and stitch together (Figure 2). Turn right side out.

Figure 2

8. Finger-press raw edge of sleeve to wrong side at gathering stitches. Slip arm into sleeve, extending past end for hand, and tightly gather sleeve (Figure 3). Hand-tack sleeve to arm. Repeat with other sleeve and arm.

Figure 3

9. Slip shirt over head and gather around neck; tack in place. Gather top of sleeve and hand-stitch a sleeve/arm to either side of shirt neck referring to sample photo. Hand-stitch shirt bottom together.

10. Tie red ribbon in a bow around the neck.

11. Referring to sample, stitch stiffened white thread through cheeks for whiskers using embroidery needle. Trim to desired length. Add a dot of glue to base of whiskers to hold in place.

12. If necessary, trim fur to ¾ inch wide. Trim hairs if too long. Stitch fur trim around mitten top.

13. Insert body into mitten up to underarm and hand-stitch to mitten. Refer to sample and tack tail and greenery in place behind the mouse.

14. Tack right arm in a down position and left arm bent and stitched only at the tip of the hand so a candy cane can be slipped through the arm.

15. To complete, rouge cheeks with watered-down red fabric paint. Add glue to eyes and teeth; let dry. Then, referring to sample, paint teeth and whites of eyes and add black pupils with a tiny white twinkle dot. *Note: If using glossy accents glaze instead of glue, add another drop to eyes after paint dries. This gives eye rounded, glossy look. Add dot of Twinkles Glitter to eye twinkle dot.*

16. Once the eyes are dry, add a wire hanger and candy cane. ■

46

Trim the Tree

Holiday Ponies

Design by Missy Shepler

Finished Size
4 inches tall (not including hanging loop)

Materials
- 1 (9 x 6-inch) rectangle lightweight felted wool
- 2 (¼–⅜-inch) buttons
- Heavyweight thread
- All-purpose thread
- Candy cane
- Small amount polyester fiberfill
- Basic sewing supplies and equipment

Materials Tip

Substitute craft wool if local fabric or quilt shop doesn't carry hand-dyed felted wool. For more visual texture, cut pieces from a variety of coordinating felted wool scraps

Cutting
Use patterns provided on insert. Transfer all markings to fabric.

From felted wool:
- Cut 2 horse heads, reverse one.
- Cut 2 ears.
- Cut 1 (⅜ x 6-inch) hanging loop strip.
- Cut 1 (1 x 9-inch) horse's mane strip.

Assembly

1. Hand- or machine-stitch along horse bridal lines and neck edges on right side of each horse head piece as marked.

2. Stitch one button on each horse head piece where marked for the eye.

3. Fold each ear in half, pinching the flat bottom edge together. Pin one ear to each horse head on wrong side at placement dots. Hand-tack base of each ear in place, making sure stitching doesn't show on the right side of head.

4. Zigzag-stitch with all-purpose thread along each long edge of hanging loop. Add decorative stitching down center of hanging loop with heavy-weight thread.

5. Fold loop in half and pin ends to wrong side of one horse head, approximately ¼–½ inch behind ear. Hand-tack the loop ends in place, making sure stitching does not show on the right side of head.

6. Gather stitch ⅛ inch from one long edge of horse's mane. Gather until the horse's mane measures 5 inches (Figure 1).

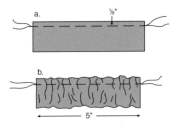

Figure 1

7. Pin gathered edge of mane to wrong side of one horse head, adjusting gathers to fit (Figure 2).

Figure 2

8. Align horse heads wrong sides together; pin. Stitch ⅛ inch from outer edge leaving the neck edge open.

9. For a sweet treat, insert the curved end of a candy cane into the horse neck before hanging or tuck a small handful of fiberfill stuffing into head to add dimension and stitch neck closed. ∎

Give Me a Paw

Design by Linda Turner Griepentrog

Finished Size
4½ x 4½ inches (excluding hanger)

Materials
- 1 each 9 x 12-inch rectangle red and white felt
- Paper-back fusible web
- ½ yard ½-inch-wide polka-dot grosgrain ribbon
- Pinking shears (optional)
- Basic sewing supplies and equipment

Cutting
Use patterns provided in insert.

From red felt:
Cut two paw socks.

From white felt:
- Trace paw pads onto fusible web backing paper. Follow manufacturer's instructions to fuse paw pads to felt.
    Cut out the individual pads following the traced lines. Do not remove paper backing.
- Cut 1 (1¼ x 6½-inch) cuff. If desired, use pinking shears to slightly trim lower edge.

Homemade Dog Treats

2 cups whole wheat flour

2 (4 ounce) jars pureed baby food*

*Check to be sure there is no onion in your flavor choice as dogs can't eat onions.

- *Preheat oven to 350 degrees.*
- *Mix the ingredients together to form a stiff dough.*
- *Roll out dough ¼ inch thick on a lightly floured surface. Cut dough into small squares or use a bone-shaped cookie cutter.*
- *Place on a lightly greased cookie sheet and bake 20 to 25 minutes. Allow treats to cool before giving to your favorite canine.*

Assembly

1. Follow manufacturer's instructions to fuse pads to paw sock front referring to photo for placement.

2. With wrong sides together, stitch around paw sock front and back ⅛ inch from edge using a narrow, short zigzag; leave upper edge open (Figure 1).

Figure 1

3. To make a hanger loop, cut a 6-inch piece of grosgrain ribbon and fold in half wrong sides together. Place ribbon ends inside paw sock at left side seam; baste in place ⅛ inch from upper edge (Figure 2).

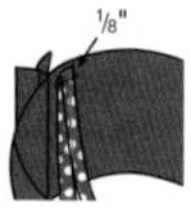

Figure 2

4. Stitch cuff short ends together to form a circle.

5. Position cuff inside sock matching side seams, with cuff right side against paw sock wrong side and hanger loop between (Figure 3). Stitch around the upper opening. Turn cuff and hanger loop to sock right side.

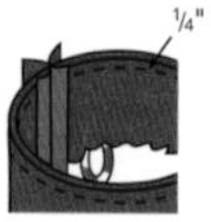

Figure 3

6. Tie a bow with the remainder of ribbon and hand-stitch at base of hanger loop. Trim ends at an angle.

7. Fill with treats for your favorite furry friend. ■

Snowman Trio

Designs by Wendy Sheppard

Finished Sizes
5½ x 7½, 4 x 5 and 4 x 4½ inches

Materials
- White/cream scraps
- Scraps for desired borders and backing
- Batting scraps
- Thread
- Pearl cotton to coordinate with borders and backings
- Scrap lengths of ribbon
- Polyester fiberfill
- Spray starch
- Buttons (optional)
- Basic sewing supplies and equipment

Cutting

From white/cream scraps:
- Cut 1 (3½ x 4½-inch) A rectangle.
- Cut 1 (4½ x 6½-inch) B rectangle.
- Cut 1 (4½ x 5-inch) C rectangle.

From border and backing scraps:
- Cut 1 each 4½ x 5-inch C, 4½ x 5½-inch A and 6 x 8-inch B backing rectangle.
- Cut 2 each 1¼ x 6½-inch D and 1¼ x 6-inch E strips.
- Cut 4 (1 x 4½-inch) F strips.

From batting scraps:
- Cut 1 each 5 x 6-inch A, 5 x 5½-inch C and 7 x 9-inch B rectangles.

Assembly
Stitch right sides together using a ¼-inch seam allowance unless otherwise indicated.

Use patterns provided on insert. Transfer all markings to fabric.

1. Apply spray starch to each of the A, B and C rectangles; let dry. Fold and crease each rectangle to mark the horizontal and vertical centers.

2. Center and transfer the Waiting for Snow Snowman motif onto the A rectangle, the It's Snowing Snowman onto the B rectangle, and the Starry Snowman onto the C rectangle.

3. Sew F strips to opposite sides and top and bottom of the A rectangle as shown in Figure 1; press seams toward strips.

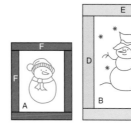

Figure 1

4. Sew D strips to opposite sides and E strips to top and bottom of the B rectangle, again referring to Figure 1; press seams toward strips.

5. Pin each rectangle to a corresponding-size piece of batting.

6. Using pearl cotton to coordinate with backing or borders, backstitch along the marked lines to complete the embroidered designs.

7. Trim batting even with the embroidered tops.

8. If adding buttons, sew to the stitched tops as desired.

9. Cut ribbon into three 6–9-inch lengths as desired; fold in half right side out to make loops. Pin and machine-baste a loop to the center top edge of each embroidered top referring to Figure 2.

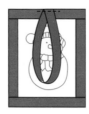

Figure 2   **Figure 3**

10. Place a corresponding-size backing piece right sides together with an embroidered top and stitch all around, leaving a 2-inch opening on the bottom edge as shown in Figure 3.

11. Clip corners and turn right side out through the opening; press flat.

12. Insert polyester fiberfill inside each stitched ornament to desired fullness.

13. Turn opening edges to the inside along seam allowance; hand-stitch in place.

14. Tie a length of ribbon into a bow around the bottom of the ribbon loop referring to the Placement Diagrams; hand-stitch a button to the bow, if desired, to finish. ■

Snowman Trio
It's Snowing Snowman Ornament
Placement Diagram 5½" x 7½"

Snowman Trio
Waiting for Snow Snowman Ornament
Placement Diagram 4" x 5"

Snowman Trio
Starry Snowman Ornament
Placement Diagram 4" x 4½"

Baby's First Christmas

Design by Chris Malone

Finished Size
4 x 5¾ inches

Materials
- Small piece felt each dark pink, orange and light blue or light pink
- 1 (9 x 12-inch) sheet white felt
- Standard embroidery floss:
  - black
  - white
  - dark pink
  - orange
  - light blue
  - light pink
- 2 black seed beads
- 8 inches of ⅛-inch-wide white satin ribbon
- Small amount polyester fiberfill stuffing
- Transfer pen (air- or water-soluble)
- Tacky fabric glue (optional)
- Freezer paper (optional)
- Basic sewing tools and equipment

Cutting
Use patterns provided on insert. Transfer all markings to fabric.

From small pieces of felt:
- Cut 2 baby buntings and 1 bow from light blue or light pink.
- Cut 1 each scarf and ½ x 4-inch scarf tail from dark pink.
- Cut 1 each large and small carrot nose from orange.

From white felt:
- Cut 2 each Snow Mamas and Snow Babies. Transfer 2014 to bottom front of one Snow Mama.

Assembly
Stitch all embroidery using two strands of floss. Refer to pages 16 and 56 for embroidery stitch diagrams.

1. Use black floss to backstitch smile and 2014 where marked on body front.

2. Pin scarf and large nose in place on body front referring to photo. Use matching floss and blanket stitch, appliqué scarf and nose to body.

3. Stitch the two beads to the face for eyes.

4. Appliqué the small nose to the baby's face with orange floss and blanket stitch referring again to photo. Use black floss to make two French knots for eyes.

5. Pin baby front and back together and blanket-stitch all around with white floss; lightly stuff the body and head as you stitch.

6. Using matching floss, blanket-stitch across top edge of two bunting pieces. Layer bunting piece; Snow Baby, head extended beyond bunting; and second bunting piece. Pin pieces together.

7. Blanket-stitch around the edges of bunting (Figure 1). Do not catch Snow Baby in stitching.

Figure 1

8. Wrap matching floss around the center of the little bow; pull to gather tightly. Knot floss; tack bow to top front of the bunting for boy or top of head for girl as shown in photo.

9. Pin Snow Mama's front and back wrong sides together and blanket-stitch all around with white floss. Lightly stuff arms, head and body as you stitch.

10. Position and attach baby on Snow Mama with glue or thread tack, as shown in photo. Fold each arm over to hold baby and tack or glue in place.

11. Blanket-stitch around all the edges of the Scarf Tail with dark pink floss. Tie a knot in the center and tack the knot to the side of the scarf front.

12. For a hanger, fold the ribbon in half and tie a knot at the end; tack to top back of head. ∎

Mr. & Mrs. Snowman

Designs by Margie Ullery

Finished Size
2¾ x 4¼ inches

Materials
- 1½-inch square orange felt
- 1½ x 2-inch black felt
- 3-inch square each red and green felt
- 6 x 10-inch piece white felt
- Buttons:
    6 tiny snowflakes
    2 tiny red hearts
    4 micro-mini black
- Standard embroidery floss to match:
    black
    green
    red
    white
    orange
- 2 (7-inch) lengths ⅛-inch-wide white ribbon
- Polyester fiberfill
- Basic sewing supplies and equipment

Cutting
Use patterns provided on insert. Transfer all markings to fabric.

From orange felt:
- Cut 2 noses.

From black felt:
- Cut 2 hats.

From red felt:
- Cut 2 bows.
- Cut 1 vest.

From green felt:
- Cut 1 each apron and hat band.

From white felt:
- Cut 4 bodies and 8 arms.

Assembly
Hand-stitch using two strands of embroidery floss for all stitching.

1. Referring to photo, stitch noses to heads of two bodies. Add black buttons for eyes and French knots below the noses for the mouth.

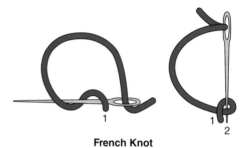

French Knot

2. Stitch a vest on one body. Attach three snowflake buttons down the middle of the vest to make the front of Mr. Snowman.

3. Stitch three snowflakes and one heart button to the bottom of the apron. Stitch the apron to the other body to make the front of Mrs. Snowman.

4. Stitch hat band to one hat and stitch a heart button to the right end of the band. Set aside.

5. Stitch arms together; leave small opening on one side. Lightly stuff and stitch arms closed. Make four arms.

6. Tack ribbon hanger loop at top of heads on wrong side of front. Stitch front and back bodies wrong sides together; leave small opening on one side. Lightly stuff and stitch closed.

7. Refer to photo and tack arms in place below head.

8. Position bow pieces on either side of Mrs. Snowman head with hanger between and stitch together.

9. Position hat pieces on front side of Mr. Snowman head with hanger between and stitch together. ■

Mr. Flurry

Design by Chris Malone

Finished Size
4½ x 6 inches

Materials
- Small piece each:
    white felt
    blue felt
    green felt
    pink felt
    orange felt
    white plush
- Standard embroidery floss to match:
    black
    white
    blue
    green
    pink
    orange
- Buttons:
    2 (¼-inch-diameter) black
    1 (¾-inch-diameter) white snowflake
- 1 small white pompom
- 8-inch-length white pearl cotton or thin cord
- Fiberfill stuffing
- Transfer pen (air- or water-soluble)
- Tacky fabric adhesive
- Basic sewing tools and equipment

Cutting
Use patterns provided on insert. Transfer all markings to fabric.

From felt pieces:
- Cut 2 white heads, 2 pink cheeks, 1 orange nose, 2 blue hats and 1 green bow tie.

From white plush:
- Cut two hat trims.

Assembly
All embroidery is worked with two strands of floss to match felt. Use patterns provided on the insert.

1. Refer to the pattern and appliqué the nose and two cheek circles onto the head using a blanket stitch.

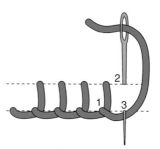

Blanket Stitch

2. Transfer the smile using an air- or water-soluble pen to the face and stitch using a stem stitch.

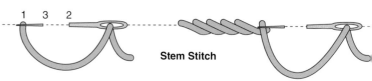

Stem Stitch

3. Sew the black buttons in place for eyes referring to the photo.

4. Pin the second head to wrong side of completed face. Work a blanket stitch all around, lightly stuffing with fiberfill before completing stitching.

5. Pin hats together and work a blanket stitch around the side edges, starting and stopping ¼-inch from the bottom corners (Figure 1). Lightly stuff the hat.

¼"   ¼"

Figure 1

6. Slip the hat bottom edge over the head top edge. Use a few dots of glue to secure.

7. Glue a hat trim piece to the hat front and back, pinching the pieces together where they meet at each side. Glue a pompom to the tip of the hat.

8. Work a blanket stitch all around the edges of the bow tie. Fold into a bow matching the narrow center sections.

9. Wrap two strands of green floss around the layered center narrow sections several times and

pull to gather (Figure 2). Knot the floss. Use floss tails to tack the bow tie to the bottom of the face.

Figure 2

10. Sew the snowflake button to the hat referring to the photo.

11. To make a hanger, thread a needle with white cord, take a small stitch into the top back of the hat and tie the cord ends in a knot. ■

Marvin the Melting Snowman

Design by Marie Darrow for Eazy Peazy Quilts

Finished Size
3 x 6 inches

Materials
- 6-inch square white felt
- 4-inch square gray felt
- 3-inch square lime green felt
- Buttons and beads:
    - 5 (¼-inch) 2-hole black buttons
    - 1 medium triangular coral bead
    - 1 medium round white bead
    - 3 flat star, single-hole beads
    - 3 red seed beads
- Thread:
    - Black 12 wt pearl cotton or 6-strand embroidery floss
- General purpose thread
- Embroidery needle
- Basic sewing supplies and equipment

Cutting
Use patterns provided on insert. Transfer all markings to fabric.

From white felt:
- Cut 2 each Body and Head pieces.

From gray felt:
- Cut 2 Snowbanks.

From lime green felt:
- Cut 2 Hat pieces.

Assembly
Refer to photo and patterns for positioning. Referring to diagram on page 56, blanket stitching is done using 36–40-inch lengths of one strand of pearl cotton or 3 strands of embroidery floss.

1. Stitch black buttons and coral bead to one head as marked for eyes and nose.

2. Blanket-stitch the head pieces together. Start stitching at top of head and finish by making a loop at base of stitch, draw the needle through to knot and bury the end between the layers; cut thread close to head.

3. Stitch star and red seed beads to one hat piece referring to photo.

4. Blanket stitch hat pieces together. Begin stitching at solid dot on left side of brim edge stitching over top of hat to opposite solid dot leaving bottom open and needle still threaded.

5. Place hat over head referring to photo and continue blanket stitching the front and back of hat to head. Knot referring to step 2.

6. Stitch three black buttons on one of the body pieces as marked.

7. Place the body pieces together. Using the pearl cotton or embroidery floss, bury a small knot close to top edge above the buttons between the layers.

8. Thread the needle through the white medium bead and then through the bottom of the face in the chin area catching a bit of wool or the base of a blanket stitch before bringing the needle back through the white bead and into the body of the snowman. Keep needle threaded.

9. Blanket-stitch completely around the body ending at the top. Knot referring to step 2.

10. Blanket-stitch flat bottom of snowbank pieces together between the solid dots leaving top open.

11. Place body inside the opening and continue blanket stitching the front and back of the snowbank to the body. Knot referring to step 2.

12. Make a loop for hanging at top of hat with pearl cotton or embroidery floss. ∎

Thready Freddy

Design by Margaret Travis for Eazy Peazy Quilts

Finished Size
3-inch diameter

Materials
- 1 (2-inch) square each black and orange felt
- 3-inch-diameter plastic foam ball
- White cotton sewing thread
- 1 ladies black crew-length sock
- 12 wt pearl cotton: red, green and black
- Embroidery needle
- 2 flat round, single-hole beads
- 2 red glass headed straight pins
- 15 inches ¼-inch-wide red satin ribbon
- Craft glue
- Mod Podge®
- Small foam disposable brush
- Aluminum foil or wax paper
- Basic sewing supplies and equipment

Assembly
1. Wrap white cotton sewing thread around the plastic foam ball, continually rotating in all directions until ball is completely covered.

2. When ball is completely covered, add a drop of white glue to secure the end of the thread.

3. Add a drop or two of water to ¼ cup Mod Podge; mix thoroughly.

4. Cover the thread ball with Mod Podge using a tapping motion with foam brush. Do not rub or swipe.

5. Allow to dry on wax paper or aluminum foil overnight.

6. To make the hat, cut horizontally across sock 3¼ to 3½ inches from the top of the sock referring to Figure 1.

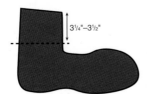

Figure 1

7. Gather up the top and tie ribbon tightly into a bow about ½ inch down from the cut edge.

8. Embellish hat band referring to photo with a row of single cross-stitch and French knot embroidery stitches using single strands of red and green pearl cotton.

Individual Cross Stitch

French Knot

9. Cut six ¼-inch squares of black felt for mouth and eyes.

10. Cut two noses using pattern provided on insert from orange felt. Layer and blanket-stitch by hand using one strand of black pearl cotton completely around nose. Refer to page 56 for Blanket Stitch diagram.

11. Position hat on dry thread ball.

12. Referring to photo, position and glue eyes, nose and mouth on ball to make face. Glue large end of nose only leaving rest of nose unglued.

13. Attach beads to eyes with glass headed straight pins referring again to photo.

14. Attach pearl cotton hanging loop to top of hat. ∎

Snowflake Duo

Designs by Charlyne Stewart

Finished Size
6 x 6-inch and 8½ x 8½-inch on the diagonal

Materials
- ⅓ yard white, sheer iridescent fabric
- ⅓ yard thin batting
- 1 spool white all-purpose thread
- 1 spool silver metallic thread
- ¼ yard pattern paper
- Fine-point blue permanent marking pen
- 24 inches ⅛-inch-wide white satin ribbon
- Large-eye needle
- Rubber cement
- File folder cardboard, tracing paper and pencil
- Sharp craft scissors
- Basic sewing supplies and equipment

Preparation & Cutting
Use patterns provided on insert. Transfer all markings to fabric.

1. Cut two 6-inch squares from the pattern paper.

2. Fold paper in half on diagonal; fold in half again and again to make an eight-layered piece as shown in Figure 1. Repeat to make a second folded piece.

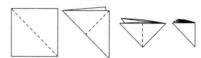

Figure 1

3. Prepare a template for each snowflake using the patterns given. Glue the template to the file folder cardboard using rubber cement; cut out.

4. Place the template on the folds of the pattern paper as shown in Figure 2; pin in place. Trace; remove template and re-pin layers. Cut out on traced lines; open paper to reveal pattern.

Figure 2

5. Cut two 6-inch squares white, sheer iridescent fabric and one 6½-inch square fleece. Pin or baste batting between fabric layers.

6. Place pattern on top of layered fabrics; pin. Trace around shape and in all open areas using fine-point blue permanent marking pen. Unpin; remove pattern.

Assembly

1. Using silver metallic thread in machine needle and white all-purpose thread in bobbin, machine-stitch on all marked lines using a medium-width zigzag stitch; repeat using a slightly wider stitch.

2. Using sharp craft scissors, cut close to stitching lines all around inside and outside edges, being careful not to cut through stitches; trim all loose threads.

3. Machine-quilt angled straight lines to simulate ice fractures referring to red lines in Figure 3.

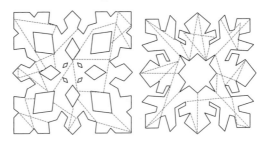

Figure 3

4. Cut the ⅛-inch-wide white satin ribbon into two 12-inch lengths. Using a large-eye needle, thread ribbon through one point of the snowflake. Tie ends in a double knot for hanging loop. ■

Snowflake Duo
Snowflake 1 Placement Diagram
6" x 6" and 8½" x 8½" on the diagonal

Snowflake Duo
Snowflake 2 Placement Diagram
6" x 6" and 8½" x 8½" on the diagonal

Let It Snow

Design by Missy Shepler

Finished Size
4 inches in diameter

Materials
- 2 (6-inch) squares light-color cotton
- 1 (5 x 12-inch) rectangle print cotton
- 1 (6-inch) square batting
- 1 (6-inch) piece ribbon or flat trim
- 1 (12-inch) piece rickrack (optional)
- 1 (18-inch) piece ribbon (optional)
- 1 each light, medium and dark shade of thread in desired color
- Basic sewing supplies and equipment

Cutting
Use patterns provided on insert. Transfer all markings to fabric.

From print:
- Cut 1 each 5 x 5½-inch and 5 x 6½-inch rectangles for backing.

Stitching Ornament Front
1. Transfer the snowflake or snow text pattern and the outer circle onto the right side of a light-color 6-inch square.

2. Layer the unmarked 6-inch square, wrong side up; batting and marked 6-inch square, right side up; pin together in each corner to secure.

3. To make the lettering or snowflake shapes stand out, free-motion quilt a small stipple stitch with the lightest shade of thread in the spaces between and around the lettering or snowflake shapes. Do not stitch into the letters or shapes.

4. Continue stitching ½ inch past the marked circle, using a looser stipple stitch as you move away from the text or shapes.

5. Switch to medium shade of thread and stipple stitch over the area again in the same manner, leaving some of the lighter stippling uncovered around the circle outer edges.

6. Repeat again with the darkest shade of thread, leaving some of the medium stippling uncovered. The letters or snowflake shapes should be very well defined and easy to read.

7. Remove pins and marking lines to complete the ornament front.

Assembly

Stitch right sides together with a ¼-inch seam allowance unless otherwise indicated.

1. Make a paper trimming window by cutting the pattern along the outer solid circle. Center the window over the stitched ornament front; carefully mark and then trim along the outer circle.

2. Fold backing rectangles wrong sides together making one each 5 x 2¾-inch and 5 x 3¼-inch rectangles (Figure 1); press. If desired, stitch a decorative machine stitch along each folded edge.

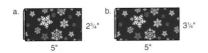

a. 2¾" 5" b. 3¼" 5"

Figure 1

3. Fold the 6-inch ribbon or flat trim piece in half forming a loop. Position and baste the ribbon ends at the front center top ⅛ inch from edge (Figure 2).

Figure 2

4. Overlap the folded edges of the backing rectangles by about ½ inch, right sides up, and smaller rectangle on top; pin or baste to hold.

5. Layer backing unit, right side up, and stitched front, wrong side up; pin. Stitch around outer edge of ornament front (Figure 3). Trim seam allowance to ⅛ inch and turn ornament right side out pulling hanger away from seam; press flat. ■

½"

Figure 3

Hanger Tip

Optional hangers can be made by twisting the rickrack together to make a flat trim (Figure A) or tying a bow in an 18-inch ribbon, leaving a loop for hanging (Figure B) and referring to the photos. Stitch the optional hangers into the ornament referring to step 3.

Figure A

Figure B

Special Thanks

Please join us in thanking the talented designers whose work is featured in this Christmas ornament collection.

To download templates for easy printing, go to: *AnniesCatalog.com/ customers/check_code.html* **and enter 151064**

Diane Bunker
Angel in Lace, page 24
Gingerbread Cheer, page 21
Mouse in a Mitten, page 44
Perky Penguin, page 40

Marie Darrow
Marvin the Melting Snowman, page 58

Linda Turner Griepentrog
Give Me a Paw, page 48
Lollipop, Lollipop, page 30
Poinsettia Perfection, page 26

Kate Laucomer
Nativity Ornaments, page 18

Chris Malone
Baby's First Christmas, page 52
Beaded Patchwork, page 34
Christmas Tussie Mussie, page 27
Clothesline Christmas Tree & Bell, page 4
Joy, page 12
Mr. Flurry, page 56
Patchwork Star, page 32
Ribbons & Taffeta, page 28
Santa & Angel Ornaments, page 13
Santa Gift-Card Holders, page 16
Tweetie Bird, page 42
Weiner Wonderland, page 37

Linda Miller
Tree-mendous Threesome, page 8

Missy Shepler
Holiday Ponies, page 47
Let It Snow, page 62

Wendy Sheppard
Snowman Trio, page 50

Charlyne Stewart
Snowflake Duo, page 60

Margaret Travis
Thready Freddy, page 59

Margie Ullery
Candy Cane Stocking, page 36
Holiday Sentiments, page 31
Mr. & Mrs. Snowman, page 54
Yo-Yo Tree & Wreath, page 7

Lynn Weglarz
Primitive Angel, page 22

Tie Dye Diva Patterns
Hexagon Wreath, page 6
Little Rudolf, page 38

Annie's® *Trim the Tree* is published by Annie's, 306 East Parr Road, Berne, IN 46711. Printed in USA. Copyright © 2014 Annie's. All rights reserved. This publication may not be reproduced in part or in whole without written permission from the publisher.

RETAIL STORES: If you would like to carry this pattern book or any other Annie's publications, visit AnniesWSL.com.

Every effort has been made to ensure that the instructions in this pattern book are complete and accurate. We cannot, however, take responsibility for human error, typographical mistakes or variations in individual work. Please visit AnniesCustomerCare.com to check for pattern updates.

ISBN: 978-1-57367-522-2
1 2 3 4 5 6 7 8 9